The Physics of Us

The Physics of Us

Poems by

Colin D. Halloran

© 2025 Colin D. Halloran. All rights reserved.
This material may not be reproduced in any form, published,
reprinted, recorded, performed, broadcast,
rewritten or redistributed without
the explicit permission of Colin D. Halloran.
All such actions are strictly prohibited by law.

Cover design by Shay Culligan
Cover image by Toa Heftiba
Author photo by Leah Nelson

ISBN: 978-1-63980-816-8

Kelsay Books
502 South 1040 East, A-119
American Fork, Utah 84003
Kelsaybooks.com

you know who you are

Acknowledgments

Thank you to the following publications, in which versions of these poems previously appeared:

Blackheart Magazine & Haiku for Lovers: "Post"

The Northeast Coast: "Let Me"

Contents

The Physics of Us	11
The First Law of Newton	12
What She Wrote	14
Invisible Rebellion	15
Because You Are a Gardener	19
Catch-22	20
Index of Refraction	21
Beirut	22
Do You Remember . . .	23
Catch and Release	24
Post	27
The Song on the Radio	28
The Second Law of Newton	30
Let Me	31
Shoulders	33
You've Got Me Thinking	34
Amateur Cartography	37
Parallax	39
Yesterday in Therapy I Realized	41
Ariadne	42
The Mythology of Snow	43
Posthumous Insomniac	46
Vanishing Point	48
Hannah Spins	49
Amateur Cartography (Reprise)	52
Black & White	53
The Third Law of Newton	54
Clocks	56
The Time I Didn't Call	57
Magellan	58

The Physics of Us

Lesson 1: Things That Fall

Rain. Leaves, in autumn.
Snow, in winter. Birds, when young.
Me, the day we met.

Lesson 2: Things That Fall Away

cancer patients' hair
old men's tired will to live
you, the day we met

The First Law of Newton

an object at rest stays at rest,
an object in motion stays in motion

You said that if you ran
it would be away from me.

So why am I surprised
to find myself alone?

Was it the *if* that I believed,
clinging to linguistic hope
the lack of certainty
found in *when*.

It's not that I don't trust you
that I didn't believe you
or didn't want to.

It's more that I believed
in us
in sunsets on the Sound

in sea glass found in shadows,
your feet just below the surface
as you raced for a balloon.

But certainty's still lacking
this love is all unknowns.
And I cling desperately
to *if*.

So wrap my heart
in concertina wire
so the harder you hold onto it
the more it's like to bleed.

Then maybe you'll absorb me
and when you run—it's clear you will—
you'll have no choice
but to bring me with you.

What She Wrote

Yesterday
I brought you to my favorite place.
We sat in the sand
until the tide lapped at our feet.
You chased me
as I zig-zagged along the shore.
We missed the sunset
when you followed me across the jetty.
I rescued a balloon off the sandbar
and you held it by the string.
We talked about birthdays
how they always fell apart.
We talked about complications
how they were inevitable.
We talked about friendships
how they were unreliable.
We talked about life
how it was so un-fucking-fair.
We talked about death
how it clung to us, even now.
We talked
about love.
& we talked about love.
We talked.
About—
love,
Love.

Invisible Rebellion

Time intersects in architecture,
the modern and young
framed in Baroque,
a quiet contradiction in the first arrondissement,
each layer a cover-up
history's whispers buried in ornament.

Do you see me?
Sentinel in the courtyard?
A complement to my surroundings
cautiously merging the then, the now,
hinting towards the next unknown.

Or do you see through me

to what I distort
some vague recollection
of happiness
or pain
refracted in my facets.

Or are you me,
mirrored in marble?

Reaching for out there
because being in here
rooted
in stone, you do not know
such beauty coexists within these walls.
Within your symmetry.

They say I let the light in.
They say you are lesser.
That you, a model, solidifying in stone
all that I am supposed to be,
and I
a window and a song,
hope in your deep-seated cell.

But at night
you
turn my panes to projectors,
announce my presence
my darkness
to the City of Light.

Your light reaching out
across courtyards
across time
across history's whispers

illuminating reflections of my self
inverted in the water's stillness,
approximating the rest of me
that hides
that reaches inward
downward
to you. Always you.

Mirrored in marble, the ringing silence of night,
a stillness unknown on the Seine this hour,
the only time we have to form new whispers
that echo out through angles intersecting
history
becoming its new secret,

realizing this existence is not silence,
not quiet contradiction.

My glass, transparent in daylight,
angles at odds
with all that surrounds me
grounded
in stone

by you.

You who sees the truth in my inversions
real and reflected.
My invisible rebellion
now ours.

Opposition in geometric form,
the new golden ratio:
one me to one you.

Because even Fibonacci could be wrong.
No remainder.
No decimals repeating.

Nothing repeating but history's secrets
coursing through my glass,
rooted in your stone.
Coursing through us

in this resistance
only you and I
can see.

Because You Are a Gardener

You saw the dirty bed,
the vines—unwanted yet unintentional—
choking the life out of everything else.
Overwhelming.

Because you are a gardener
you saw me
not just as I was but as I could be.

You took the time, the care
the tenderness, the time—so much time
to nurture. To care.

Now I, too, know
I'm only just beginning to blossom.

Catch-22

We know the rock
the hard place

the false choice.

Dichotomies have always lied.

Because there is not a me
or a you.

There is not an us.

There is just this.

This moment.
This being.

This seeming truth, which

seen closer

is as false as the choice
we thought
we
started with.

Index of Refraction

And the way the streetlight hit the water
became a brilliant metaphor
as the orange light became a fire
dancing just beneath the surface
breaking, occasionally, to replenish its fuel.

Two contending forces coexisting,
this reflection gave me hope,
beautiful, even if it is a lie,
because really metaphors are just calling
something what it's not
and maybe the dance was less a dance
than a struggle.

But I know that after I leave—
and until the sun overpowers it—
that flame will dance on, at just the right angle,
embracing its brief existence
just beneath the surface.

Beirut

I wanted to go home with you
to see Beirut through those olive eyes
learn about you
as you learned about your past
in that city more war torn
than even me

I wanted to be
even just a minor character
in the memoir you were writing
for ink
and paper
to bind us together
for more than just those moments we had
when we were both pulled in other directions
when we were nothing but potential.

Do You Remember . . .

When you jumped the fence
into the orchard
and, finally out of your grief,
you said it just might be
time for fireworks.

That hillside where you first said
you loved me
surrounded by a stranger's
peach trees,
the Sound in sight.

The way you'd throw back
your head
and laugh
and laugh
      and laugh
as we cruised down the Merritt.

The way our rainy Sunday afternoons
made me question
every day's forecast.

Catch and Release

And I was surprised

by the gentle touch of your
calloused fingertips
as they worked across my back

pads the roughest I've felt
and yet they soothed.

No surprise

the soft touch, nimble weaving
required
to attach a fly to a line

to cast and catch
a salmon in the highlands

a heart on an island

a shard of a soul.

You cast
and caught

me.

An island of a soul
turned malleable:
clay and heart in your hands.

. . . and lead us not into temptation . . ..

But you did.
Didn't you.

Did you know what you
set out to do?

To plant
to nourish

hope.

Then harvest.

The scythe of your words
the chaff of my heart
my hope

dead

piled onto a fire

and burned

the way my heart
my hope
had burned for you.

But now . . .

empty smoke

rising

to an empty heaven.

Post

Lying next to you
I do not feel you, only
that you are not her

The Song on the Radio

said "I miss your purple hair
I miss the way you taste."
And I do.

Driving from Connecticut
to Johnstown in a car that
had no business going that far,
you taught me about the flood
and thoughts of you have flooded
me since.

You introduced me
to my favorite band,
the one that saved me summer
after senior year.
Songs taken off albums
and rearranged on CD-RW
in an order you said made you
think of me.

And now every time I see them
I think of you,
wonder if you still spell
confusion with a k.

And I'll always remember
where I was when Strom Thurmond died,
which isn't at all romantic,

but I was in your arms
when that racist bastard kicked the bucket
so when his filibuster record is broken
I think of you.

Of your purple hair.
Of how quick we closed
the distances between us
and of just how little time
we actually had.

The Second Law of Newton

the acceleration of an object depends on the mass of the object and the amount of force applied

Met with the silence
of my unanswered question still hanging
in the air

I attempt to answer
for you

Imagine

what you might have said:

it was as real as anything else.

And now my optimism
has me seeking ghosts

anything that isn't there

more questions

I cannot bear to answer.

Because if this
if us
was as real as everything
around me

I need to live in illusion.

Let Me

Let me be there
your rock
like the one we thought was a seal
off St. Mary's by the Sea.

Let me be there
when the world makes you think you're crazy
mad
unable to stand on your own.

Let me be there
to tell you
you can.

You can be crazy.
You can stand on your own.

But let me be there
if you choose not to.

Choose me
to be there, your rock—constant.

Choose me
to open up to
to crash your frustrations up against
like so many waves on the jetty
we use to block the wind
light our cigarettes.

Choose me.
And let me.

Let me be vulnerable.
Let me open myself to you
as I never dreamed I could.

Let me bare my being to you.
And let yours be borne to me.

Choose
to be me.
And let me
be you.

Shoulders

I cannot remember
the last time I woke
to such a sight.

Or I don't want to.

Why, when the breeze
off the sea mirrors
me embracing you,
would I let my mind go elsewhere?

But the breeze can see
all of you; I can only see
your shoulder.

Soft as the call
of the fog horn across
three nautical miles

it is more beacon
than warning to turn
away. I hope
you will not turn back
to face me
hiding bare shoulders.

You've Got Me Thinking

The sun sets
Not because it doesn't like the day
or wants to give the moon a chance
(they sometimes share the sky)
It may be simple nature,
Being.
Setting is what suns were sent to do,
But westward movements
lead it back around the rose
and so, perhaps, I am no son.

I've always wanted to write
a poem including dinosaurs
achievements
and alchemy
and here, once more, a chance
for growth
for existence
for the fact
reptilian types tend toward eating
in migratory manners
moving on when sustenance was emptied.

But lush greens still exist here
so a dinosaur I'm not
though they told me that
when I grew up
I could be anything.

But not everything.

And so Costa Rican coffees bear
a richer
smoother
taste

history
oil
sweetness
enacting their magic
or science
on this dark
dark liquid I take
into my soul
my stomach,
acidic

tearing away enamel
and peace of mind.

But that is not the point.

In Costa Rica beans are picked—
no, berries—
berries are picked
not by automation
automatons
but by men
who know
who sense
the richness of the red

the discrimination toward ripeness
picked each day by hand

while those in
Colombia
are mechanized

no discerning
ripe from rare
unready from red.

Amateur Cartography

The shortest distance between two points is love. Or a line, geometrically speaking. For example, if point A is in Carolina—no, you should be point A—if point A is in California, and point B is in Carolina, however strong that love is, geometrically speaking, a line is needed. I stand on one side of a continent, you on the opposite edge, same continent. The ground we stand on is supposed to be the shortest distance. And yet I do not feel connected until my toes touch the sea.

I want to draw you a map. Show you the mountains, the vast expanse, the toll roads, ravines. All obstacles. All making a straight line irrelevant. *Then fly*, they'll say. But you hate airports and I don't do large crowds. We each have our demons. We each have a past.

But *our* past—those shared points in time, where the shortest distance between two points is zero—that is on the shore. Your shore or mine, such distinctions don't matter, geometrically speaking. I heard once that space is curved. Like the Earth. Like the brim of the hat I clumsily bump against your forehead when I lean in for a kiss on a shore that's almost a year away.

So I let my heels sink into the continent as the waves bring me closer to you. Because there are two lines between these points. And when I touch the ocean, and I know you're touching that other ocean, I know that we're together. Connected. Once more one point contained in two bodies. It is the longer line, geometrically speaking, but it is undoubtedly ours.

And when I touch the ocean, and I know you're touching that other ocean, and I know those oceans, somewhere, meet, this continent—with its mountains, its ravines and vast expanses—is just a dock. And it's like I'm back there. On our shore. With you. Sitting on our dock, your feet hanging off one side, mine the other, leaning back against each other, one point—in space, in water, in time—connected.

Parallax

I was in your hometown today
Without you—
It goes without saying—
Not visiting, just passing though
A 3-minute stop at the station
Between another here and there.

The thing about travelling by train is
The things that are close blur
But faraway things stay clear, still.

I heard you're in the capital now—
Or maybe it was farther north—
But I bet your parents are still here
In their house with Christmas mornings,
A wood fire stove, football.

I wonder if your ring
Has joined your high school swim trophies
In their attic. Or if it's gone.

I know that now there's little feet
And laughter of children
That aren't mine.
And I wonder if your girls
And my girls
Would be friends
Or if the hurt we gave each other
Somehow passed to them.

I looked for the restaurants we used to go to
I tried to recognize a beach we walked on once
But the view from the tracks is limited
My memory even more so.

And now I'm facing backwards
Watching the tracks I came on curve away
Into the marine layer
Disappearing
Like memories
Like you
Like us

Yesterday in Therapy I Realized

I have these feelings
but I don't know what they are

or how to tell you

that I don't know

how to feel
or at least how to define them

that I don't see

the world the way that you do
or the way I feel I should

that I can't see

a way out for myself
that doesn't involve a grave

or isolation

because what I feel is
a grave

calling me to its loving embrace

but I know that's not
how feelings are supposed to work

but I don't know how they should

Ariadne

I could not drown,
For Bacchus loved her well,
So I tried and tried to burn.

The Mythology of Snow

Do you know how hard it is
to follow the flight of a single flake
released from some unseen start
meandering
among millions
to its final place of rest,
identity receding once more
into the anonymity of oneness.

Do you know how hard it is
just to find a flake, its singularity,
meandering geometrics
tessellating endlessly in our imagination
that word
unique
that lie we know so well.

Monet and Turner knew this to be true,
Impressionism
the new Realism
in this splintering reality,
how is it only they and I
and you
could see.

Hanging in the Minneapolis Institute of Art
the eyes of Beard's owls
exude a desperation
driven on by bearded winter's whip

which must be made of wind
because no matter how much time
I spend in scrutiny
I cannot seem to find it.

In New York City Francois Boucher's
fourth season
calls out across time
and memory
a pink cloak, fur-lined,
a mill, surely stopped, its river frozen,
though all things are on canvas.

And surely, there was a man,
pushing the pink-cloak's sleigh,
but he is not clear,
not like her skin, white as Beard's owls,
he is blurred, blinded by memory
by time
by me, relegated to a shadow,
Turner's train.

Which is to say
that even the greats
could not capture that singular flake
just the knowledge that it surely must exist
somewhere

in memory
in time
in countless allegories of swirling winds
and mills that stopped their turning.

Somewhere between creation
the fall—more allegory—a final
blanket, impermanent rest
science tells us a singularity exists
just one
of each.

If only for a moment.

Posthumous Insomniac

for Molly

You once asked
if death felt like insomnia,
settling into a room with too-low ceilings.
And I wish you didn't know.
I wish you didn't need an answer so badly.
But you were never satisfied
with simply wondering—
too determined for that.
You needed certainty.

You said it was always insomnia
that brought the most clarity
that brought you closest to God,
when creativity flourished
and doubts fell away.

Insomnia made you feel
that the world's ceilings were too low,
but unlike Whitman's multitudes
you could not be contained.
Your smile and spirit,
your soaring soul.

And now I'm left to this.
Walls and ceiling
closing in around me
constricting me like the lungs in my chest

wondering what would have happened
if I'd ignored her and answered
that late night call.
And all I can do
is send my words

my love
my sinking soul

out into the ether.

Vanishing Point

as the sun sets to my right
my eyes gaze straight ahead
there's nothing on my mind
but what's behind me

Hannah Spins

She dances palindromatic
like her name
weaving in and weaving out
beautiful both ways.

Even backwards, she always
made sense.
Even in reverse
the story begins with love.

Even after the end
we knew we'd always
have the middle.

And in the middle
Hannah dances.

She throws back her head
and smiles a smile that means the music
is surely drowning
out her laughter—
or she's breathing in the notes.

The melody sustains her.

My favorite picture:
you took my camera while I was driving,
open top Jeep in what must have been
the summer air

my hands at 10 and you.
Holding it out with both arms
you snapped exhilaration,
teenage joy with hair akimbo.
That night we would break
curfew.

Or the time we skipped school
and crossed state lines to get our
first tattoos. Twenty years ago;
your mom still won't forgive me.

Or the sapphire ring
you told your sister was a family heirloom,
some obscure great aunt.

You couldn't bear to give it back.

Because even in reverse
the story starts with love.

Playing it back from start to end
I see you spin. Head back, laughing.
Undoubtedly in love.

But in reverse I see
beyond that. Head tilted,
looking back to see
your shadow self waiting

for the next dance
for the chance to be free
for that same exhilaration
for hair tossed not by wind

but by the first dance with your wife
who spins you into joy.

Amateur Cartography
(Reprise)

I want to draw you a map.

The shortest distance between two points
you
me

an answer not found in textbooks

me
you

the shortest distance between two points

I want to draw you a map
of my dreams.

Black & White

You sent me a picture
of your new tattoo—
forget-me-nots—
as if I ever could.

The Third Law of Newton

whenever one object exerts a force on another object
the second object exerts an equal and opposite on the first

How do I separate
your pain
from my heart?
My words
from your desires?
My desires from your thoughts?

The weight
and flutter
unfelt for so long
a simultaneous undoing:
weight and weightlessness at once.

But I question
the way the universe seems balanced
complete
a realm of matching pieces.

Is my being weightless your weight
your pain
transferred and transcribed
heavy as my words
my desires
your thoughts?

This is the trouble with balance
with understanding
with knowing
each piece must have its inverse.

Where some see puzzles
I see contradiction
completion.
Fear.

I doubt.

Not because I want to,
not because I doubt you,
but because I doubt myself

my words
my desires.

Clocks

And I wish I could write this
in the present tense.
But our story fell victim
to the grammar of time.

The Time I Didn't Call

I knew the perfect words to break you
their exact weight
their precise point of impact
the memories they'd conjure

even with the words unspoken
I can hear them
in the echoes of your haunted heart

and that's enough
to stop me.

Magellan

I take comfort
in knowing the world
is round.

Every step you take
as you walk away
brings you
one step closer to me.

About the Author

Colin D. Halloran is the author of three collections of poetry: *Shortly Thereafter, Icarian Flux,* and *American Etiquette*. He holds an MFA from Fairfield University.

Halloran received a Ph.D. from Old Dominion University, where he studied war as a cultural object. His dissertation, The War Poetry Map Project, is a digital humanities project that engages with 20th and 21st century warfare through poetry and cartography.

Website: www.colindhalloran.com
Socials: @poetinpinkshoes

www.ingramcontent.com/pod-product-compliance
Lightning Source LLC
Chambersburg PA
CBHW030915170426
43193CB00009BA/856